Discover Castles

by Katrina Streza

© 2017 by Katrina Streza
ISBN: 978-1-53240-205-0
eISBN: 978-1-53240-206-7
Images licensed from Fotolia.com
All rights reserved.
No portion of this book may be reproduced
without express permission of the publisher.
First Edition
Published in the United States by
Xist Publishing
www.xistpublishing.com
PO Box 61593 Irvine, CA 92602

2

To get to the castle, we need to walk past the knight.

4

To get to the castle, we have to cross the moat.

To get in the castle, we have to cross the drawbridge.

To get in the castle, we have

8

to walk under the gate.

To get in the castle, we have to find the doors.

To get through the doors, we need to find the key.

To use the key, we need to find the lock.

To get through the castle, we need to walk past the window.

To get through the castle, we need to walk past the castle flag.

To get through the castle, we need to walk past the dungeon.

20

To get through the castle, we need to walk past the kitchen.

To get through the castle, we need to walk by the knight in a suit of armor.

To get through the castle, we need to walk up the stairs.

To get through the castle, we need to walk by the throne.

To get through the castle, we need to walk by the crown.

There is so much to see in the castle!

33

www.ingramcontent.com/pod-product-compliance
Lightning Source LLC
LaVergne TN
LVHW010020070426
835507LV00001B/18